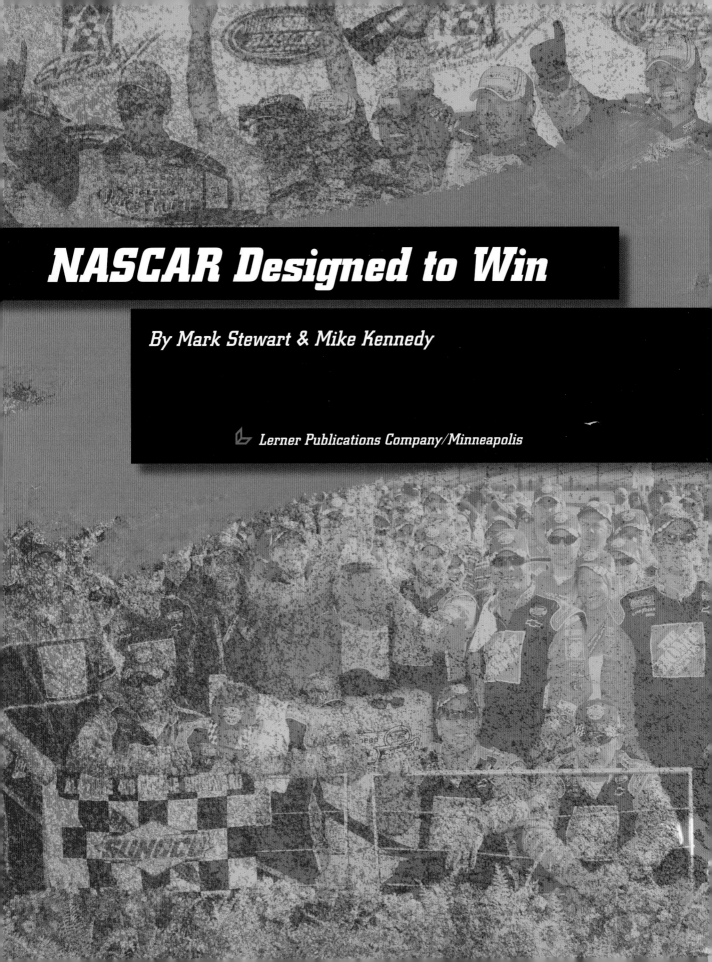

NASCAR Designed to Win

By Mark Stewart & Mike Kennedy

Lerner Publications Company/Minneapolis

The publisher wishes to thank science teachers Amy K. Tilmont and Jeffrey R. Garside of
the Rumson Country Day School in Rumson, New Jersey, for their help in preparing this book.

Lerner Publications Company
A division of Lerner Publishing Group, Inc.
241 First Avenue North
Minneapolis, MN 55401 U.S.A.

Website address: www.lernerbooks.com

All photos provided by Getty Images.

Library of Congress Cataloging-in-Publication Data

Stewart, Mark, 1960-
NASCAR designed to win/by Mark Stewart & Mike Kennedy.
p. cm. -- (The science of NASCAR)
Includes index.
ISBN 978-0-8225-8736-1 (lib. bdg. : alk. paper)
1. Stock car racing—United States—Juvenile literature. 2. NASCAR (Association)—Juvenile literature.
3. Stock cars (Automobiles)—Maintenance and repair—Juvenile literature. I. Kennedy, Mike (Mike
William), 1965-
II. Title.
GV1029.9.S74S7475 2008
796.72–dc22   2007033861

Manufactured in the United States of America
1 2 3 4 5 6 – DP – 13 12 11 10 09 08

Contents

Introduction   **4**

Chapter One: Inside the Ride   **6**

Chapter Two: Outer Limits   **14**

Chapter Three: Driven to Win   **22**

Chapter Four: The Money Game   **30**

Chapter Five: The Road to Victory   **38**

Glossary   **46**

Learn More   **47**

Index   **48**

What does it take to build a successful racing team? NASCAR team members are always looking for ways to make their car a little bit better, a little bit faster.

This book looks at the building blocks of a winning team—from the car to the driver to the people who pay the bills. It also takes you through a NASCAR race, from practice runs and qualifying races to raising the winning trophy on Victory Lane.

EVERY PERSON ON A NASCAR RACING TEAM HAS AN IMPORTANT JOB TO DO.

LEFT: CREW CHIEF LARRY CARTER *(LEFT)* AND DRIVER JAMIE MCMURRAY WATCH QUALIFYING RUNS FOR A 2007 RACE IN NEW HAMPSHIRE.

ABOVE: MATT KENSETH *(RIGHT OF SURFBOARD)* CELEBRATES A VICTORY WITH HIS ENTIRE TEAM.

In the early days of NASCAR, the cars zooming around the track were called stock cars. This was because they looked just like the cars that were "in stock" at local car dealerships. Many fans went to the track and rooted for their family car to win!

Back then, the main differences between race cars and family cars were under the hood. NASCAR drivers and mechanics knew how to squeeze extra power out of the engines. Over the years, they also learned how to improve the performance of every other part of a car.

JEFF GORDON'S CAR MAY NOT LOOK LIKE A FAMILY CAR, BUT IT IS STILL CALLED A STOCK CAR.

By Design

Modern stock cars and family cars have almost nothing in common. The need for speed and the focus on safety have led to major changes in NASCAR vehicles inside and out.

THE LOOK OF RACING HAS CHANGED OVER THE YEARS. *TOP:* THREE CARS STEER THROUGH A TURN IN A RACE FROM THE 1960s. *ABOVE LEFT:* KASEY KAHNE BUCKLES HIMSELF INTO A MODERN RACE CAR. *ABOVE RIGHT:* RICHARD PETTY WAS A STAR IN THE 1960s, 1970s, AND 1980s.

Motor Works

The engines that power NASCAR vehicles have eight cylinders. These are shaped like tall soup cans. Inside each cylinder is a piston that can move up and down. Hoses push a mixture of fuel and air into the cylinder. A spark from a spark plug lights the fuel-air mixture. The mixture explodes, or combusts. The combustion forces the piston to move downward. This downward stroke transfers power to the engine.

With all eight cylinders working together, the engine gets a steady supply of explosive power. The power turns a long rod that leads to the rear axle. The axle transfers energy to the rear wheels. The rear wheels push a race car along the track. The front wheels are connected to the steering column. A driver controls the direction of the car with the steering wheel.

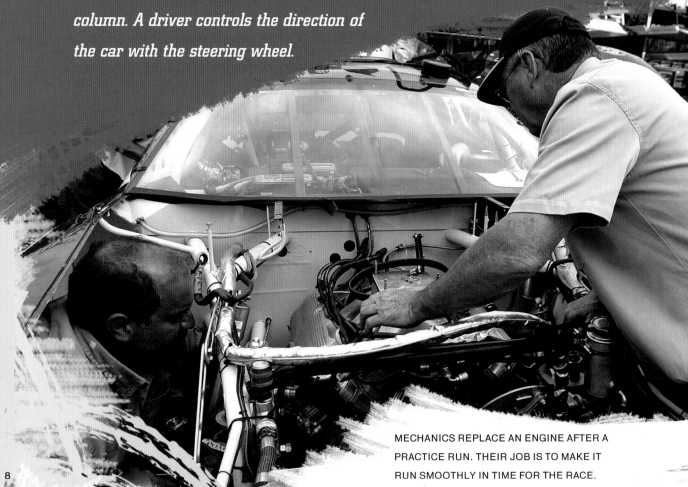

MECHANICS REPLACE AN ENGINE AFTER A PRACTICE RUN. THEIR JOB IS TO MAKE IT RUN SMOOTHLY IN TIME FOR THE RACE.

In the Mix

NASCAR engines use 110-octane fuel. The fuel at your neighborhood gas station is between 87 and 93 octane. The higher the octane rating, the more power the car has.

ABOVE: AN ENGINE HEADS TO THE GARAGE AFTER A PRACTICE RUN AT THE DAYTONA 500 IN FLORIDA. *TOP:* THIS ENGINE USES HIGH-OCTANE FUEL TO POWER A DODGE CHARGER RACE CAR.

Speeding toward the Future

Every part of an engine does something to make a car run smoother or go faster. If one part is not working well or is made poorly, a car can slow down. For many years, NASCAR mechanics built racing engines piece by piece. This way, they could control the quality of every part.

But engines soon became more complicated. Making everything by hand became very difficult and expensive. A single engine might cost more than $50,000. Beginning in the early 2000s, NASCAR started to develop the Car of Tomorrow (COT). Its engine is powerful, reliable, and less expensive than the hand-built ones. Starting in 2008, every team built its engine to the new design.

KYLE BUSCH WAVES THE CHECKERED VICTORY FLAG ON HIS WAY TO VICTORY LANE AT BRISTOL MOTOR SPEEDWAY IN TENNESSEE. BUSCH WAS THE FIRST TO WIN A RACE DRIVING THE CAR OF TOMORROW.

By Design

If an engine runs too hot, it can fail. NASCAR's COT design brings cooling air into the engine from under the front bumper. In old designs, air came through the front grille, which could get clogged with dirt or garbage.

TOP: A CREW CHANGES ENGINES IN A COT. THE NEW ENGINES ARE LESS EXPENSIVE THAN THE OLD HAND-BUILT ONES. *ABOVE:* TONY STEWART WAITS IN HIS COT WHILE A MEMBER OF HIS CREW CHECKS HIS ENGINE. STEWART WAS ONE OF THE DRIVERS TESTING NASCAR'S NEW DESIGN.

See for Yourself

Engines don't just need fuel. They need oil too. Motor oil keeps the parts that rub against one another—through friction—from heating up and wearing out. To see why this is important, try the following experiment.

- Hold a plastic pen in each hand. Rub the pens together as fast as you can, as if you were starting a fire with two sticks.
- After 30 seconds, touch one of the pens to your lips. You can feel how warm it has become.
- Dribble a few drops of cooking oil onto a napkin. Lightly coat both pens.
- Rub the pens together again for 30 seconds. Check the temperature of the pens again. They are much cooler than before because the oil has reduced the amount of friction.

Coating engine parts with motor oil keeps them from wearing out at high temperatures by reducing the friction.

Powerful Blend

NASCAR engines have carburetors, where air and fuel are mixed. Hoses then move the mixture to the cylinder where combustion takes place. The more air that is pulled into the mixture, the more power the engine can produce. Modern passenger cars no longer use carburetors. They use fuel-injection systems instead. Of course, these cars don't run at 180 miles per hour. Carburetors are still the best option for racing engines.

Shoptalk

"TO PUT IT SIMPLY, NASCAR TEAMS CAN GET MORE HORSEPOWER FROM AN ENGINE WITH A CARBURETOR THAN WITH FUEL INJECTION."

—DRIVER MARK MARTIN

EXPERIENCED DRIVERS LIKE MARK MARTIN (ABOVE), TONY STEWART (No. 20), AND BILL ELLIOTT (No. 21) LIKE THE EXTRA POWER THEY GET FROM ENGINES THAT USE CARBURETORS.

Over the years, car builders shaped their designs to be as smooth as possible. This meant the cars had no parts that resisted (pushed against) the air. Car designers learned how to make the air help them go fast and remain under control in traffic. Cars began racing close behind one another in single file. Air passed over the entire line of cars. This racing tactic is called drafting. Drafting gave drivers fewer reasons to pass.

But racing fans love passing. NASCAR wanted to encourage drivers to pass more often. So NASCAR engineers studied the way air flows over and around a car's body. This study is the science of aerodynamics. NASCAR designers made several changes to the outside of the cars. Their goal was to create a shape that would make passing easier.

TWO LINES OF CARS DRAFT AT
HOMESTEAD-MIAMI SPEEDWAY IN FLORIDA.

ONE OF THE DIFFERENCES BETWEEN MATT KENSETH'S COT (*No.17*) AND RICHARD PETTY'S CAR OF THE 1980s (*No. 43*) IS HOW THEY CUT THROUGH THE AIR AT HIGH SPEEDS.

Do the Math

Fans love to see changes in which car is leading a race. Let's say the leaders change once every 10 laps in a 200-lap race. How many lead changes are there altogether?

(answer on page 48)

Winds of Change

To please fans, NASCAR always looks for new ways to challenge drivers. So NASCAR designers changed the shape of the cars to create more air resistance. For example, the front windshield was tilted up slightly. The front bumper was redesigned to catch more air than before. These aerodynamic changes have tested the skill of drivers. Teams must try many different ways to win. NASCAR races are more exciting than ever!

SMALL CHANGES IN NASCAR'S DESIGN MAKE A
BIG DIFFERENCE TO DRIVERS LIKE KASEY KAHNE *(ABOVE)*.

ABOVE: A NASCAR OFFICIAL LOOKS AT THE SPECIAL TEMPLATE USED TO TEST THE SHAPE OF THE COT. BELOW: A REAR WING CREATES DOWNFORCE AND HELPS CARS STAY ON THE TRACK.

Show of Force

In some cases, air resistance can help a driver go faster. A car's rear wing sits on the back of the car. It is angled to catch the air and push down the rear of the car. This is called downforce. Downforce improves the grip, or friction, of the rear tires on the track. Stronger friction gives the driver more control at high speeds and during turns.

Handled with Care

Another goal of NASCAR engineers was to design cars that were easier to handle. They shaped the cars so that swirling air wouldn't move cars around as much. This change makes it easier for drivers to go through traffic.

To make cars more stable, engineers widened the rear wing. A wider rear wing increases the amount of air pressure pushing down on the back of the car. More air pressure stops the back of the car from moving side to side.

KYLE BUSCH SKIDS TOWARD THE EDGE OF THE TRACK. NASCAR'S NEW CAR DESIGN HELPS TO KEEP THIS FROM HAPPENING.

Do the Math

Let's say a crew chief orders four rear wings at the start of a season and then makes two more orders of four by the end of the season. How many rear wings has the crew chief ordered?

(answer on page 48)

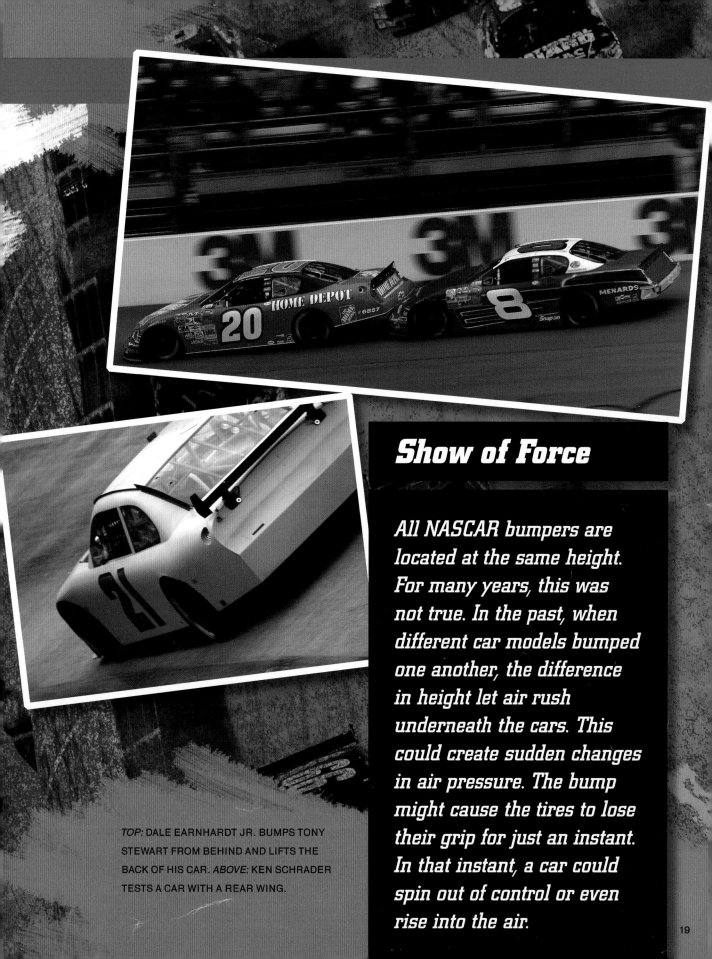

Show of Force

All NASCAR bumpers are located at the same height. For many years, this was not true. In the past, when different car models bumped one another, the difference in height let air rush underneath the cars. This could create sudden changes in air pressure. The bump might cause the tires to lose their grip for just an instant. In that instant, a car could spin out of control or even rise into the air.

TOP: DALE EARNHARDT JR. BUMPS TONY STEWART FROM BEHIND AND LIFTS THE BACK OF HIS CAR. *ABOVE:* KEN SCHRADER TESTS A CAR WITH A REAR WING.

See for Yourself

How does air pressure push an object up or down? The next time you go to a playground, wear a baseball-style cap and try this experiment to find out. (Hang on with both hands during this experiment. Never swing one-handed.)

- Pick an empty swing and start swinging. Wear the bill of your cap pointing straight out—not too high and not too low.
- After you have reached a steady speed, notice how the air flows around the bill of your cap when you swing forward.
- To increase the air pressure above your cap and decrease it below, tilt your chin down to your chest.
- You should feel the higher pressure pushing your cap down toward the bridge of your nose.
- Next, tilt your head back and your chin up, increasing the pressure below the bill of your cap and decreasing it above.

Did your hat rise up? Did it fly off? These are the basic aerodynamic forces that NASCAR teams deal with every day.

Test Day

NASCAR's COT was used in all races starting in 2008. But drivers tested the new design in several races in 2007. The results were excellent. Drivers passed more often. The design seemed to bring back more old-school racing. Also, the races were very close. Winning often came right down to the final lap.

Shoptalk

"IT PUTS THINGS BACK INTO THE DRIVER'S HANDS MORE."

—DRIVER JEFF GREEN, ON THE COT DESIGN

ABOVE: JUAN PABLO MONTOYA TESTS ONE OF NASCAR'S NEW DESIGNS. *RIGHT:* JEFF GREEN LIKES THE FEEL OF THE COT.

Chapter Three: Driven to Win

Most NASCAR fans have a favorite driver. They like that driver's skill on the track and personality off the track. No two drivers are alike. Some drivers are daring and emotional. Others take few chances and think carefully about everything they say and do.

In building a winner, a racing team looks for a driver whose skills and personality will blend with everyone involved in the team. Drivers are the ones behind the wheel on race day. But they are like one cylinder in an eight-cylinder engine. If all the members of the team aren't working well together, then the chance of winning is slim.

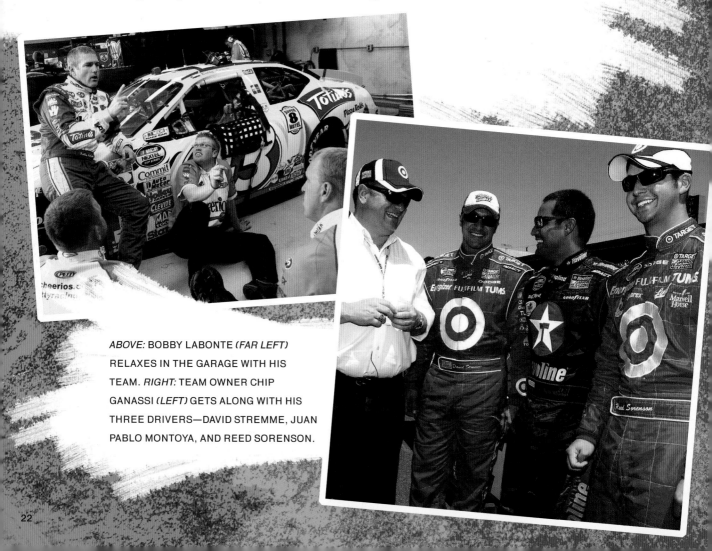

ABOVE: BOBBY LABONTE (FAR LEFT) RELAXES IN THE GARAGE WITH HIS TEAM. RIGHT: TEAM OWNER CHIP GANASSI (LEFT) GETS ALONG WITH HIS THREE DRIVERS—DAVID STREMME, JUAN PABLO MONTOYA, AND REED SORENSON.

In the Mix

Kurt Busch loved to do math in school. He also loved hard science like physics and chemistry. If Busch had fallen short of his dream to be a driver, he planned to be a scientist.

TOP: TWO FANS ROOT FOR THEIR FAVORITE DRIVERS. *ABOVE:* KURT BUSCH IS ONE OF MANY DRIVERS WHO LOVES THE SCIENCE OF RACING.

One Step at a Time

For all of their many differences, NASCAR drivers have one important thing in common. They work their way up to the top of the racing world one level at a time. Most begin before they are teenagers, racing small but powerful go-karts. From there, many graduate to midget racing (a racing class that uses small race cars). At these levels, drivers learn many of the lessons they will need to move up the racing ladder.

Talented drivers rise through several levels of stock car racing. They begin on short, local tracks. The best young drivers keep moving up. If they're really skilled, they can go all the way to the top level—the NASCAR Sprint Cup Series. Drivers, crew members, and mechanics also must prove they can be part of a winning team at each level before moving up.

TWO DRIVERS IN MIDGET CARS COMPETE ON A DIRT TRACK. FOR MANY DRIVERS, THIS IS ONE OF THE FIRST STEPS TOWARD NASCAR.

ABOVE: GO-KARTS MAY LOOK SMALL, BUT THEY ARE VERY POWERFUL. *LEFT:* JEFF GORDON WAS A GO-KART CHAMPION.

Show of Force

As a child, Jeff Gordon raced go-karts against older kids and adults. He weighed less than the other drivers. His weight didn't slow down his vehicle. His go-kart got up to speed quickly. Gordon used this advantage to win the national championship at the age of 11.

Ready to Race

Drivers who make it to NASCAR's top level have put in the time and hard work to understand every part of racing. They can take apart a car and put it back together again. Their team members know they have what it takes to drive for a NASCAR Sprint Cup Series championship.

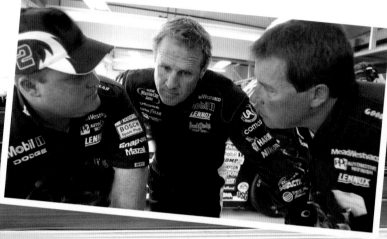

ABOVE: A. J. ALLMENDINGER (84) IS ONE OF THE NEWER DRIVERS IN NASCAR. HE MUST SHOW HIS TEAMMATES AND THE OTHER DRIVERS THAT HE IS READY. *TOP:* RUSTY WALLACE *(MIDDLE)* KNEW HIS CAR INSIDE AND OUT. HE WON 55 RACES DURING HIS CAREER.

Body Language

COMPUTERS HELP ENGINEERS FIND WAYS TO MAKE DRIVERS SAFER AND MORE COMFORTABLE.

Fans say NASCAR is the hottest ride in sports. And they aren't kidding! Drivers compete in temperatures that soar to more than 100 degrees. NASCAR engineers have helped cool things down a bit. They rerouted the exhaust system away from the driver. This system carries away the heat from burned gas.

YOUNG DRIVERS LIKE MATT KENSETH (*LEFT*) MUST LEARN TO STAY COOL WHEN THE TEMPERATURE RISES

See for Yourself

NASCAR drivers have to be aware of their surroundings. They must also take action quickly when they spot danger or a chance to take the lead. But they have to avoid making a mistake. How difficult is this? To get an idea, try this experiment.

- Find two old tennis balls or rubber balls. Go outdoors.
- Stand one giant step away from a solid, flat wall that has no windows.
- Using one hand, gently throw one ball underhand against the wall. Catch it with the same hand.
- Do the same with the ball in your other hand.
- Do this a few times with each hand until you can do so without dropping the balls.
- Try the same action, but before you catch a ball with one hand, flip the other ball against the wall.
- Keep repeating this action so that you are never holding more than one ball at a time.

How long can you keep the balls in motion without dropping a ball? Like driving in a NASCAR event, this experiment demands that you watch two things at once. You have to have good control between your hands and your eyes to make quick moves. And most of all, you need to practice a lot!

Chasing Points

A NASCAR season has 36 races. NASCAR awards points for each race. No race is worth more points than any other. So drivers must try hard every week to win. The number of points awarded depends on where the drivers finish. They also get points for how many laps they led during the race.

After 26 races, the 12 drivers with the most points spend the final 10 races competing for the NASCAR Sprint Cup Series championship. This is called the Chase for the NASCAR Sprint Cup. Any driver can win those specific races. But only the top 12 drivers are in the Chase and can win the championship.

ShopTalk

"IF YOU'RE NOT IN THE CHASE, YOU'RE A NOBODY. THOSE ARE KIND OF HARSH WORDS, BUT THAT'S WHAT EVERYBODY WANTS. YOU GET RECOGNIZED. THEY TALK ABOUT YOU. YOU'RE PART OF THE SERIES."

—DRIVER GREG BIFFLE

TOP RIGHT: JIMMIE JOHNSON RAISES THE TROPHY HE WON FOR BEING THE 2006 NASCAR SPRINT CUP SERIES CHAMPION. *ABOVE:* GREG BIFFLE FINISHED SECOND IN THE 2005 CHASE FOR THE NASCAR SPRINT CUP.

Chapter Four: The Money Game

Building a winning team is very expensive. A team owner must pay the salaries of drivers, mechanics, and crew members. Money is needed for new cars, engines, and parts. A team owner also pays for the living expenses of employees while they are on the road. A NASCAR season is about 10 months long. So that's a lot of money!

ABOVE: TEAM OWNER ROBERT YATES (RIGHT) TALKS TO HIS DRIVER RICKY RUDD. RIGHT: JOE GIBBS IS A FAMOUS NFL FOOTBALL COACH, AS WELL AS A NASCAR TEAM OWNER.

The cost of owning a NASCAR team is about $10 million a year. This doesn't even count the salary of the driver. An owner can save some money by having more than one team. The teams can share some jobs and expenses. But each team is still very expensive.

LEFT: TEAM OWNER RICK HENDRICK (*LEFT*) SHARES THE JOY AND GLORY OF WINNING THE NASCAR SPRINT CUP SERIES TROPHY IN 2006 WITH DRIVER JIMMIE JOHNSON.
ABOVE: RICHARD CHILDRESS OWNS TEAMS AT SEVERAL LEVELS OF NASCAR.

Paying the Bills

How can anyone afford to build a winning NASCAR team? In the early days of racing, the companies that made stock cars gave teams a lot of money. The companies knew that having a winning image would help them sell cars to racing fans. For example, if a Ford car won a race on Sunday, Ford dealers would sell a lot of cars the following week.

These car companies still support NASCAR teams. But team owners get most of their money from sponsors. These are companies that want to have their name connected with a winner. The names of sponsors cover almost every part of a car.

THE HOME DEPOT SPONSORED
TONY STEWART'S CAR IN 2007.
M&M'S SPONSORED DAVID GILLILAND'S CAR.

ABOVE: A WIND TUNNEL IS A GOOD WAY TO TEST THE AERODYNAMICS OF A CAR. BELOW: SCOTT PRUETT DRIVES A CAR SPONSORED BY JUICY FRUIT GUM.

Show of Force

Carmakers can still support a NASCAR team. They can let a team use the company's wind tunnel. These are special labs that test how air moves around a car. Testing cars in a wind tunnel gives teams information about aerodynamics they cannot get on the track.

Logo Mania

Superstars such as Jeff Gordon and Tony Stewart may drive the cars, but NASCAR sponsors drive the sport. The main sponsor of a successful team pays $5 million or more to put its name on the hood of the car. The name is in big letters, where all the fans can see it. The sponsor also puts its name on the driver's uniform. The special label a company uses is called its logo.

Many sponsors give special bonuses (extra money) to teams that do well. Even if a car doesn't win, the team can still earn a bonus if the car leads the race for a number of laps. This is because all eyes are on the leader. That means more eyes on the sponsors' names and logos.

THE NAMES OF MAJOR SPONSORS
CAN BE SEEN ON THE HOOD OF EACH CAR.

KEVIN HARVICK'S CAR (*ABOVE*) IS
COVERED IN LOGOS. JEFF GORDON
(*BELOW*) AND TONY STEWART (*RIGHT*)
MAKE SURE THEY ARE SEEN WEARING
THE NAMES OF THEIR SPONSORS.

Do the Math

Let's say Kevin Harvick's
car has 27 company
logos on each side. A
total of six more cover
the hood and the trunk.
What is the total number
of logos on the car?

(*answer on page 48*)

See for Yourself

Wind tunnels are large and complicated. But the basic idea is very simple. NASCAR teams want to understand how air flows around different parts of a car at high speeds. Try this experiment to see a little of what the engineers do.

- Find a Ping-Pong ball. Ask permission to use your family's handheld hair dryer.
- Turn on the dryer to the cool setting. Point the airstream directly upward.
- Hold the Ping-Pong ball about three inches above the opening. Then quickly release it.
- Because the edges of the ball are perfectly curved, the air will flow around it evenly and hold it in place.
- Gently nudge the ball with you finger. The airflow will quickly nudge it back!

A wind tunnel blows air at a car in the same way. Every angle, edge, and curve on the car's body changes the airflow.

King Carl

NASCAR's first great team owner was Carl Kiekhaefer. He owned a successful company that made motors for boats. In 1955, he started a NASCAR team to advertise his company. Kiekhaefer could pay for the best cars, equipment, mechanics, and drivers. Kiekhaefer hired six different drivers in 1955. They won 22 of the 45 races held that year.

Shoptalk

"CARL TOOK ME OUT OF THE KITCHEN EATING HAMBURGER AND PUT ME IN THE DINING ROOM EATING STEAK!"

—DRIVER BUCK BAKER, WHO WON THE NASCAR SPRINT CUP SERIES CHAMPIONSHIP IN 1956 AND 1957 DRIVING FOR CARL KIEKHAEFER

CARL KIEKHAEFER (*LEFT*) POSES WITH THREE OF HIS DRIVERS. HIS DRIVERS WERE THE FIRST TO WEAR TEAM UNIFORMS.

Chapter Five: The Road to Victory

The final steps needed to build a winner are the same at each race. When a team arrives, workers unload the car off a truck. Team members set up the garage. Mechanics prepare the car for its first practice run. This preparation includes changing the car's suspension system to match the track. The mechanics choose the tires they believe will work best.

Do the Math

Let's say three mechanics work 40 minutes each on an engine. What is the total number of hours they have spent working on the engine?

(answer on page 48)

KEVIN HARVICK'S CREW PREPARES HIS CAR FOR ITS FIRST PRACTICE RUN BEFORE THE SHARPIE 500 AT THE BRISTOL MOTOR SPEEDWAY.

Practice runs are very important. Sometimes everything will feel perfect to the driver the first time around. Usually small changes need to be made. Mechanics, engineers, and specialists discuss new ideas with the driver, the crew chief, and the team owner. The car needs to be perfect for the next step—the qualifying run.

TOP: THE GARAGE AREA IS BUSY AT BRISTOL MOTOR SPEEDWAY. *ABOVE:* A NASCAR OFFICIAL USES A TEMPLATE TO CHECK THE SHAPE OF BRIAN VICKERS' CAR BEFORE A RACE.

By Design

Before and after the practice period, teams must let NASCAR officials inspect (look at) their cars. NASCAR inspectors check each car's size, weight, and shape. They test its engine. They make another inspection right before the real race begins. These reviews are to make sure that all cars are following NASCAR's rules. NASCAR doesn't want any car to have an unfair advantage in a race.

Beat the Clock

Qualifying runs usually take place two days before the real race. Each car must complete two laps around the track at full speed. The faster lap is the one that counts. The faster the qualifying speed, the closer to the front a driver starts. The fastest qualifier earns the pole position. This is in the front row on the inside, or shortest, part of the track. The pole position is the best spot on the track.

Qualifying runs are very exciting to watch. Only one car is on the track at a time. The driver pushes the car to go as fast as it possibly can without losing control. The speeds during qualifying runs are much faster than speeds on race day. This is because the car only has to make two laps, not hundreds of laps.

SCOTT RIGGS TAKES HIS CAR ON A QUALIFYING RUN.

JEFF GORDON FOCUSES ON THE JOB AHEAD. HE IS GETTING READY FOR HIS QUALIFYING RUN AT THE SYLVANIA 300 AT NEW HAMPSHIRE INTERNATIONAL SPEEDWAY.

Do the Math

At the 2007 Daytona 500, 61 cars made qualifying runs. Only 43 were allowed to start. How many teams were not able to compete in the race?

(answer on page 48)

NASCAR races usually are held on Sundays. That's the end of a long and tiring week for racing teams. But for fans, race day is a huge event. Drivers and crews feed off fan energy. Still, to win a NASCAR race, everything must go exactly right.

The car has to be running well. A driver must avoid accidents. Pit stops need to be quick and clean. A winning team must have a smart strategy. Perhaps it'll take a chance or two and hope that luck is on its side. If all of this happens, the car may zoom across the finish line first.

TONY STEWART SHOWS OFF HIS TROPHY
FOR WINNING THE 2007 ALLSTATE 400 IN INDIANAPOLIS,
INDIANA. HE'S CELEBRATING THE VICTORY WITH HIS HOME DEPOT TEAMMATES.

Do the Math

The two NASCAR drivers with the most career victories are Richard Petty and David Pearson. Petty has 200. Pearson has 105. What is the total number of victories for these two drivers?

(answer on page 48)

TOP: KYLE BUSCH HAS ONLY A FEW FEET TO GO BEFORE CROSSING THE FINISH LINE FIRST. *ABOVE:* RICHARD PETTY CROSSED IT FIRST 200 TIMES IN HIS CAREER.

See for Yourself

Sometimes the difference between winning and losing comes down to small changes during a race. Maybe a driver feels a car is out of balance. The pit crew can improve its speed and handling by changing the pressure on one of the springs. To see the difference this makes, try this experiment.

- Lace up a pair of sneakers with removable innersoles.
- Pick two landmarks outside (trees or lampposts will do).
- Ask a friend to time you as you run around both landmarks three times. You need to finish where you started.
- While you catch your breath, remove one of the innersoles. Put your shoe back on.
- Run the identical course again, and check your time.

In most cases, your time for the second run will be slower than the first. The change in balance affects the other parts of your "engine" and reduces your speed.

A Team Effort

When a NASCAR team wins a race, everyone goes a little crazy. The crew members hug one another and leap in the air. They run toward their driver jumping and laughing. Everyone meets in Victory Lane, a small stage. Here the winning team celebrates, and the race trophy is awarded. Every NASCAR driver dreams of standing on Victory Lane at the end of the day.

Shoptalk

"YOU CAN RUN A GOOD RACE AND FINISH SECOND, BUT IT'S ONLY A GREAT RACE IF YOU WIN."

—DRIVER GEOFFREY BODINE

ABOVE RIGHT: GREG BIFFLE (*ARMS RAISED*) SHARES THE STAGE WITH HIS CREW AFTER WINNING THE LIFELOCK 400 AT KANSAS SPEEDWAY.
ABOVE : GEOFFREY BODINE WON 18 RACES DURING HIS CAREER.

Glossary

aerodynamics: the study of how air flows around an object

air pressure: the weight of air on a race car

air resistance: the force of air on an object moving through it

downforce: air pushing down on a car as it moves forward. Downforce helps a car's tires stay on the track during turns.

drafting: racing closely in single file to reduce the effect of air resistance. At high speeds, drafting can lower the amount of energy needed to keep up a certain speed.

exhaust system: the pipes that take the heated air used by the engine away from a car

friction: tthe force that slows down objects when they rub against one another

horsepower: a measurement of the power of an engine

lap: one circuit around a track; to be ahead of another car by one entire circuit of the track

midget racing: a class of racing that uses small race cars

passing: going by a moving car to get in front of it

pole position: at the start of a race, the front, inside spot on the track. This position gives an advantage to the driver.

practice run: a circuit of a race track that helps a racing team test how its car might perform in an actual race

qualifying run: a race for the fastest speed. The fastest qualifier gets the pole position.

rear wing: a device at the back of a race car that helps create downforce

specialist: a person who is an expert on one part of a race car. Every team gets advice from tire specialists and engine specialists.

stock car: in early racing, a race car that was somewhat the same as a vehicle made for everyday driving

suspension system: the springs, shocks, and other parts that are used to suspend (hang) a car's frame, body, and engine above the wheels

wind tunnel: a special lab that shows how air will move around a car in a real race

Learn More

Books

Buckley, James. *NASCAR*. New York: DK Eyewitness Books, 2005.

Buckley, James. *Speedway Superstars*. Pleasantville, NY: Reader's Digest, 2004.

Doeden, Matt. *Stock Cars*. Minneapolis: Lerner Publications Company, 2007.

Fielden, Greg. *NASCAR Chronicle*. Lincolnwood, IL: Publications International, Ltd., 2003.

Savage, Jeff. *Dale Earnhardt Jr.* Minneapolis: Lerner Publications Company, 2006.

Sporting News. *NASCAR Record & Fact Book*. Charlotte, NC: Sporting News, 2007.

Woods, Bob. *The Greatest Races*. Pleasantville, NY: Reader's Digest, 2004.

Woods, Bob. *NASCAR Pit Pass: Behind the Scenes of NASCAR*. Pleasantville, NY: Reader's Digest, 2005.

Website and Video Game

NASCAR
http://www.nascar.com
NASCAR.com is the official site of NASCAR. From here you can find information on drivers and their teams, as well as previews of upcoming races, schedules, and a look back at NASCAR's history.

NASCAR 2008. Video game. Redwood City, CA: EA Sports, 2008.
With an ESRB rating of E for "everyone," this game gives fans a chance to experience the speed and thrills of driving in a NASCAR race.

Index

aerodynamics, 14, 15, 16, 20, 33
air pressure, 18–20
air resistance, 14, 16, 17

Bristol Motor Speedway, 10, 38, 39
bumpers, 16, 19

carburetors, 13
car design, 7, 14, 16–18
Car of Tomorrow (COT), 10–11, 17, 21
crew chiefs, 5, 39

Daytona 500, 9, 41
downforce, 17
drafting, 14

eight-cylinder engine, 8, 22
engineers, 14, 18, 27, 39
engines, 6, 8–13

fans, 6, 14, 16, 22, 27, 42
friction, 12, 17
fuel, 9, 12

go-karts, 24–25

mechanics, 6, 8, 10, 24, 30, 38–39
midget racing, 24

NASCAR designers, 14, 18.
  See also car design

NASCAR drivers: Allmendinger, A. J., 26;
  Biffle, Greg, 29; Busch, Kurt, 23; Busch,
  Kyle, 10; Earnhardt, Dale, Jr., 19; Elliott,
  Bill, 13; Gordon, Jeff, 6, 33–34; Green,
  Jeff, 21, 25; Harvick, Kevin, 35, 38;
  Johnson, Jimmie, 29; Kahne, Kasey, 7;
  Kenseth, Matt, 15, 27; Labonte, Bobby,
  22; Martin, Mark, 13; McMurray,
  Jamie, 5; Montoya, Juan Pablo, 21, 22;
  Pearson, David, 43; Petty, Richard, 7, 15,
  43; Pruett, Scott, 33; Riggs, Scott, 40;
  Schrader, Ken, 19; Stewart, Tony, 11,
  13, 19, 32–34, 42
NASCAR Sprint Cup Series
  championship, 24, 29, 37

passing, 14
pole position, 40
practice runs, 4, 8, 9, 38–39

qualifying runs, 4, 39–41

racing teams, 4, 16, 22, 30–32
rear wings, 17, 18, 19

sponsors, 32–33
stock cars, 6–7, 24, 32

team owners, 22, 30, 31, 37, 39

Victory Lane, 4, 46

wind tunnel, 33, 36

Do the Math Answers

Page 15: 20 laps. 200 laps ÷ 10 laps per lead = 20 laps.

Page 18: 12 rear wings. 4 rear wings x 3 orders = 12 rear wings.

Page 35: 60 logos. 27 logos + 27 logos + 6 logos = 60 logos.

Page 38: 2 hours. 3 mechanics x 40 minutes = 120 minutes. 120 minutes = 2 hours.

Page 41: 18 cars. 61 cars – 43 cars = 18 cars.

Page 43: 305 races. 200 races + 105 races = 305 races.